"PRAY TELL, PRIVATE HELL"

Published by Hellbound Press
Printed in the United States of America
First Edition--First Printing, March 2007

Library of Congress
Cataloging-in-Publication data:
Bartel, Steven
Pray Tell, Private Hell
1. History--Military & Social Life
2. The American Civil War
3. Poetry

ISBN13: 978-0-9794236-0-4

Library of Congress
Control No: 2007924513

DEDICATED
TO THE
AMERICAN SOLDIER
LIVING AND DEAD

AND TO
BRIAN C. POHANKA
1955-2005
&
ROBERT E. HAIBER
1953-2006:

AUTHORS, HISTORIANS & HUMAN BEINGS
-PAR EXCELLENCE-

"Forward!"

At Fredericksburg, Virginia, on a December day in 1862, Union General Orlando M. Poe watched spellbound as rank upon rank of his Federal comrades marched to their doom. The slope of Marye's Heights was strewn with blueclad bodies, but the survivors pressed on-- closing the gaps, bayonets fixed and flags held high-- in a virtually suicidal assault on the Rebel position. "Their devotion transcended anything I have ever seen, or even dreamed of," Poe wrote after the battle; "Men walked right up to their deaths as though it were to a feast." From his vantage point on the other side of the lines, the great Confederate commander Robert E. Lee echoed Poe's mingled sense of awe and horror as he observed the pageantry of slaughter. "It is well war is so frightful," Lee is said to have remarked, "else we should grow too fond of it."

The grim reality of killing fields like Fredericksburg was overlaid by the trappings of nobility, of honor, of romanticism-- all the "pride, pomp and circumstance" of mid-19th century expectations of what war was supposed to be. And, viewed from a distance, or with detachment, those engagements were an awe-inspiring spectacle, a panoramic canvas come to life. But the common soldier-- the pawn in that great chess game of History -- has down through the ages manifested a well-nigh universal tendency to dispense with such notions. Once the Yanks and Rebs of our Civil War had "seen the elephant"-- their euphemism for baptism by fire-- they generally left the recitation of glorious deeds to bombastic generals, newspapermen and novelists. Capable of transcendent, self-sacrificial acts of heroism-- for country, regiment, comrades, ideals-- they were at the same time gritty realists, if not cynics. They may have marched quite willingly to the feast, but knew that it was a cannibal feast.

Soldiers were perpetually dirty, hungry, homesick and generally resentful of drills, inspections and all manner of military frippery. In the words of Captain Oliver Wendell Holmes of the 20th Massachusetts Infantry: "War when you are at it is horrible and dull... an organized bore." In later decades, Justice Holmes, like many another veteran, came to exalt the lessons of his Civil War experience-- to draw from that ordeal of suffering and blood some eternal lesson and inspiration. But such thoughts, Holmes well knew, were rare indeed amidst the grungy bivouacs of the ravaged Old Dominion in the bitter years of '61 to '65.

Certainly no one who peruses the soldierly verses in this volume could mistake Pvt. Hell for a romanticist of the profession of arms, though the beauty of nature is not lost on him as he slogs his way through perdition, war holds no glory-- only devastation, pain, and a bitter irony. Like most soldiers he makes the best of what he has, which often isn't much. He savors those humble pleasures of a tin cup full of coffee, the rare meal more wholesome than army-issue salt pork, puffs on his pipe, and quaffs of the occasional flask of "Oh Be Joyful." He does not tolerate fools gladly, scorns all manner of affectation, and despises pomposity and posturing. It thus comes as no surprise that as a rule the good Private is more than a tad skeptical of officers, and downright contemptuous of politicians. He may be prone to grumbling, true, but he also displays a wry sense of humor, even if his smile is at times more akin to a grimace.

As I read these collected works of Private Hell, another author-veteran of that war came immediately to mind-- one whose brutal realism was in large degree comprised of dark-humored amusement at the grotesqueries of the battlefield, war being "a by-product of the arts of peace," as he put it. I don't know if the two ever met, but I suspect the shade of Ambrose Bierce will be most appreciative of the Private's endeavor, though "Bitter Bierce" might object to a certain vestigial sentimentality that preserves Hell from unremittent cynicism. In pondering the Private's work I thought, too, of Wilfred Owen-- the doomed English officer-poet of the First World War-- who once described the Western Front as "a place where death becomes absurd and life absurder." The dark ironies of war are sadly timeless. As Mark Twain, himself a reluctant Civil War soldier, once remarked, "History doesn't repeat itself, but it rhymes."

It should be noted that the Private's opus would not likely have seen the light of day were it not for the diligent labors of editor S. B. Bartel, who expended much time and effort tracking down and reassembling a widely scattered body of work. In discussing this project with the editor, I was interested to learn that two of Mr. Bartel's ancestors fought and bled in Hell's war. His great-great-grandfather, Swiss-born Jacob Schwab, was wounded three times during his service with the 12th U.S. Infantry; and his thrice-great-uncle, Alonzo Hayden, was killed at Gettysburg, battling in the bullet-torn ranks of the 1st Minnesota Volunteers. That legacy was doubtless of no small value in enabling the editor to establish what I trust will be his subject's posthumous place in the literary pantheon of The Tragic Era.

--Brian C. Pohanka
Alexandria, Virginia

Editor's Note

While one does not usually associate the American Civil War (1861-5) with the animal kingdom, excepting of course horses and cattle, this collection of poetry concerning that most horrible and poignant conflict unleashes upon the public a veritable menagerie-- in addition to beasts of the requisite equine and bovine ilk, the reader will encounter dogs, cats, chickens, fleas, rats, worms, swine, mules, fishes, lice, mockingbirds, a dove, a stork, an old hare, and an unruly elephant. (What, no flies?) The editor hopes that the appearance of so many animals will not unduly intrude upon the reader's Civil War reveries, if any.

Then, there's the death. There is altogether too much death in this volume, and yet, what are we to do about it? Folks herein are either dead, dying, soon to die, lamenting death, embracing death, defying death, or attempting to hasten the shuffling off of some other soul's mortal coil. Such was the age. In at least one instance, soldiers are blown to smithereens before our eyes. (Look away, look away.) Even the bones may be heard to speak. When Stephen Crane called the war "The Great Death," it would seem Private Hell's ear was cocked.

Also, it needs be mentioned that there is a 'General Disregard' for authority, particularly of the military stripe, to be found 'spoiling' this barrel, as it were, and the reader is advised to be on guard for a rather marked cynicism concerning the glory that is War.

Still, there is something to be said for many of the poems. They are short. They rhyme nicely. They are historically accurate. (As a special rejoinder, imputations by some that a brace of these compositions suffers from salacious overtones are greatly exaggerated.)

So pull up a chair, or a log, pour yourself a dollop of "O Be Joyful," and consider what Private Hell aptly described as "this vast misjudgment."

--S. B. Bartel

--Contents--

At Auction

Master Brooke and Master Hubbard
herewith bid you see their wares:
if you own no human beings,
pray buy you one of theirs.

They have ten as likely Negroes
as you have ever seen
to be auctioned at their office,
Monday, May sixteen.

-Slaves will be sold separately or in lots, as best
suits the purchaser. Sale held rain or shine--

-Pvt. Hell

*Masters Brooke and Hubbard were slavers who always had
a way with words, and their business establishment was located
in Richmond, Virginia, before the war. The industry as a whole
would suffer serious reverses during the mid-1860's. -Ed.*

To Arms

To Arms! The broadside cried, To Arms!
Now leave your cities, towns and farms
Forsake your sweetheart's tender charms
The Enemy Awaits! To Arms!

Two Arms! I once did have two arms!
Until I reached Virginia's farms
and found myself a world of harms…
I'll do with one, no more to arms!

-*Pvt. Hell*

Behold The Minié

Behold! The lowly Minié ball!
This modest lump of lead,
no bigger than my fingertip
but colder than the dead.
It knows no earthly station
of laurel, rank, or birth...
of the heart it seeks to shatter
it cannot judge the worth.
And when its bloody job is done
it will not feel the pain...
but as my dust returns to dust
'tis the Minié will remain.

-Pvt. Hell

The first modern aerodynamic bullet, the Minié ball was invented by French Captain Claude-Etienne Minié in the 1840's and greatly improved the accuracy of rifled muskets, to the delight of the man behind the muzzle and the general dismay of those in front. -Ed.

Gee! Haw!

In this steam-powered conflagration,
an affair quite full of hot gases,
it would seem the team of each nation
is led by men stubborn as asses.

-Pvt. Hell

*'Gee' and 'Haw' are the traditional mule drivers'
  commands for right and left, as given to the mule. -Ed.*

En Garde

The pen is mightier than the sword--
what, then, is mightier than the gun?
To save your soul beseech the Lord...
to save your life, you'd better run.

-Pvt. Hell

Remarkably, the lowly Private quotes Sir E.G. Bulwer-Lytton (he of the "dark and stormy night") in this poem's opening line, which Mencken dates to 1838... but surely Bulwer-Lytton himself was sucking from the teat of Martin Parker, who wrote in 1641: "More danger comes by the quill than by the sword." -Ed.

The Cavalryman's Prayer

I raise this saber in anger,
and possibly in haste--
are we to cut the mystic cords
and lay the land to waste?
A fever has us all, it seems
all eyes are burning red--
what horrors do we visit thus
upon our country's head?
I raise this saber in anger,
may God direct its course…
and God, since you are on my side,
I'll need a better horse.

-Pvt. Hell

The armies would ultimately 'use up' hundreds of thousands of horses each year, and in an extreme example, Rebel cavalry Gen'l. Nathan Bedford Forrest had no less than 29 horses killed under him in battle, (yet certainly evened the score by slaying some 30 Union soldiers in personal combat during the course of the war.) -Ed.

Salt Pork Hamlet

To kill,
or not to kill.
That is the question.

To kill,
or be killed.
That is the answer.

-Pvt. Hell

*"...I think the soliloquy in Hamlet commencing 'O, my offense
is rank' surpasses that commencing 'To be, or not to be.'
But pardon this small attempt at criticism."
-A. Lincoln, (in a letter to James Hackett, a prominent
Shakespearean actor of the day.)*

The soliloquy to which Lincoln refers concerns fratricidal murder. -Ed.

The Last Shot

I am shot! Oh God, please take me quick--
I don't want to go where you go if you're sick.
Oh the blood! I can feel it seep down my shirt
but it's odd in the way that it doesn't hurt.
And is this aroma the smell of death?
That's strange-- it's so like a saloon-keeper's breath,
and the growing stain is not red, I see...
why, my flask took the ball that was meant for me!
Oh be joyful! For life is very sweet...
too bad my whiskey's gone to St. Pete.

-Pvt. Hell

General Demise

He looks the same as any other man
now that they've stripped him of his uniform
and made off with his brand-new riding boots
and timepiece, sword, and flask that kept him warm.

He was just recently a General--
those golden stars like money in the bank…
but now he's naked as the simple truth
that Death holds no great awe for any rank.

-Pvt. Hell

Limerick's Lad

There was a young Irishman pale
From Limerick town he did sail....
Soon he shouldered a gun--
Said he: "What have I done?
Now I'm riding on Lucifer's tail!"

-Pvt. Hell

*While the lad of this poem may feel he got more than he bargained for,
the men of fair Limerick had for many generations hired out as
mercenaries to various European despots (sometimes on opposing sides)
and it was their custom to meet after a battle, exchange their trademark
5-line 'riffs' and give each man his dew, so to speak. Immigrants from
Eire-land constituted a significant proportion of the fighting forces
of both Rebel- and Yankee-dom, many regiments being almost
completely composed of Sons of Erin. On several occasions, Irish units
opposing one another nearly wiped each other out. -Ed.*

Beelzebub's Pachyderm On Parade

I dreamed I saw an elephant
trampling hither and yon…
his tusks great bloody bayonets,
his eyes blazed like the dawn.
And oh! His trunk! A mighty club
shaped like a musket-stock--
the years of war now gone before
did not reduce my shock.
He seemed to trumpet through the smoke
a sound of nations dying…
and if I wasn't scared quite dead,
'twas not his lack of trying.

-Pvt. Hell

'Seeing the elephant' was the common 19th Century euphemism
for suffering any larger-than-life experience. The immortal "Jumbo"
of London Zoo and P.T. Barnum fame ('Umjumba' is Bantu for
elephant) was originally captured as a calf in Africa in 1861. -Ed.

Gentlemens' Agreement

There is no place for gentlemen in war--
which is not noble, but it's true.
And who can say what gentlemen are for,
except to cause such fever-dreams to brew?

Ah, gentlemen-- you are a special breed,
apart from us and yet so near...
and as we march and fight and retch and bleed
we know you guard us ever, from the rear.

-Pvt. Hell

"Wisdom is better than weapons of war:
but one sinner destroyeth much good."

-Ecclesiastes 9:18 (Steel-Clad Version)

Venus And Mercury

Now down here in Washington City
is a place (where you ought not to go)
which is known as 'Hooker's Division'
'tis an Amazon army, though.

Just imagine a giant encampment
with row upon row of soiled doves
all ready to give to a soldier
the kind of attention he loves.

So stay you away from Canal Street
and the corner of 13th and D
where saloons and low sporting houses
are just about all you can see.

For a night spent with Venus, I tell you,
no matter how pleasant she be,
can lead to a lifetime with Mercury
and reduction to rank misery.

Rather, get you on up to the 'Haystack'
run by lovely Madam (Mrs.) Hays--
for her 12th Street 'delights' are the finest,
and you'll wish you could dally for days.

-Pvt. Hell

*Medical treatments for 'ailments of Venus' in the mid-1800s
included administration of the element Mercury to the sore
afflicted. Washington, DC, with more than 400 bawdy
houses, saw 24,000 arrests for prostitution in 1863. -Ed.*

Colonel Popcorn

We'd follow our Colonel anywhere
just out of curiosity…
he's such a glorious study
in pompous grandiosity,
and always fills our ears full
of luminous verbosity!
If only he'd a little of
the requisite ferocity.

-Pvt. Hell

Owed To A Canteen

You are a silly-looking jug
more fit for schoolboy's shoulder,
and yet it's you I have to lug
if I am to grow older.

Come fill the cup at break of day,
then onward to the slaughter…
for millions live without love, they say,
but nary a one without water.

-Pvt. Hell

At First Sight

Sixty-one Springfield, you're my first love,
I ain't never been with a girl--
but from your muzzle to your nipple
you are my own in this world.
With rifling as lovely as Chantilly lace
and trigger so warm and supple,
you've taught me what it is to love…
and Yanks? We've banged a couple!

-Pvt. Hell

The 1861 Springfield 'rifled musket' and its British cousin, the
Enfield, were the backbone weapons of Civil War armies. The
musket was loaded from the front end (muzzle) of its rifled
(internally spiral-grooved) barrel, and a small explosive 'cap'
was fitted to a 'nipple' on the firing mechanism near the trigger,
replacing the old 'flint' technology. So intense became the demand
for weapons as the triggers "warmed" that many flintlock-type
muskets were retrofitted for 'percussion cap' firing. Enterprising
soldiers would additionally discover that the barrel could hold
exactly one pint of whiskey. -Ed.

Base Instincts

There's this game we call 'Base,' it's played with a ball--
and it's all the 'hot spit' in camp.
There's a 'hurler' who throws at a man with a 'bat'
who must whack it, or bear its stamp!
And if he fends off this assault with dispatch
he can give that ball 'leagues to roam,'
and sprint round the great 'diamond' of bases...
(be it ever so humble, there's no base like home.)

-Pvt. Hell

Ironically, it was the War Between the States which drove
our beloved Baseball into the very marrow of the nation, and
spread it among the men from all the states, and all classes, where
it would eventually supplant fratricide as the national pastime. -Ed.

An Army Doesn't March On Its Stomach

I hope these brogans will hold out--
they're not a pretty sight.
My toes can tell the temperature
late in the frosty night.

The heels have ground to sawdust now,
the hobnails worn down clean…
just how to save my mortal soles
remains yet to be seen.

-Pvt. Hell

*Shoes, and lack of them, were a common enemy of both armies.
(The 'gunboats' of the day were often made without regard to left
or right foot ergonomic considerations.) After several years of
fighting, southern soldiery in particular was rough-shod, and many
dead Union troops gave up their soles to the vicissitudes of war.
It is often said that the Battle of Gettysburg was precipitated by a
belief that shoes were warehoused in the town. The lowly Private,
had he been so inclined, would have no doubt extended apologies
to Gen'l Napoleon for the irreverent title of this ditty. -Ed.*

Fighting Irish

Well, I had me a row with O'Leary
and I got me own in, I should say--
but he gave with a roundhouse that took me front teeth
and you can't bite a cartridge that way.
So now they are shipping me home, boys--
sure as sin won't that train be a sight,
for I've given me smile for me country!
Guess the Rebs can rest easy tonight.

-Pvt. Hell

In the early days of the war, neither army would recruit men who could not bite the end off a paper cartridge loaded with gunpowder and ball, with which to load a musket. As the conflict wore on, any man who was spry would have found himself assigned somewhere, incisors aside. -Ed.

Do No Harm, or, The Manual of Arms

For all my surgical training's good
I should have practiced sawing wood....
There are no doctors on this field,
we're carpenters, too tired to yield,
who disassemble God's design.
(By now I'd rather cut off mine
than take another soldier's hand
or arm or leg on which to stand)
I've hundreds here, in ghastly heaps
outside the door... Hippocrates weeps.

-Pvt. Hell

To Jonathan Letterman, Surgeon General, Army of the Potomac

Amputations were the most common (75%) of all Civil War surgeries, and were usually performed al fresco, taking only minutes when the surgeon was experienced. If surgery occured within 48 hours after the wounding, survival was twice as likely... but antiseptic theory, alas, had yet to be embraced by the medical community at large, and many of the wounded suffered from repeated, successively more daunting surgeries. -Ed.

A Pile of Miles

So, surgeon, go ahead and take my leg--
it's marched a pile of miles so it won't beg.
Been up and down some mountains I could name
and stood me well when Hell unleashed her flame.
But time runs out, this limb and I must part...
we promise not to run-- Be still my heart!
I recollect back home down on the farm
when I was just a lad and meant no harm,
I gave a shot of whiskey to the cow...
Good Lord, I sure could use that whiskey now.

-Pvt. Hell

Although both ether and chloroform had become commonly used
anesthetics, supplies of these libations of Morpheus, not surprisingly,
were often unable to keep up with demand. Many were the Minié
balls which bore the teeth marks of clenched determination. -Ed.

Backward Christian Soldiers

Backward Christian soldiers, marching off to War
Where's the cross of Jesus? It's been sold before...
Christ, the Royal Master-- has this man a foe?
Satan is the enemy, not your brother Joe!
Backward, Christian soldiers, march not off to War--
Would the cross of Jesus stood for something more.

-Pvt. Hell

Richard the Lionheart's men sang the rousing battle hymn
"Wood Of The Cross" as they marched off to the Holy Land
in the Second Crusade, 1191 A.D., but Private Hell and his
fellow crusaders would likely have been more familiar with their
own era's "Onward Christian Soldiers," written by the Reverend
Sabine Baring-Gould, a prolific historian, theologian, and travel
writer, not long after he was ordained into the Church of England
at Cambridge in 1861. His lyric was eventually set to the martial
strains of "St. Gertrude," composed by the inimitable Sir Arthur
Sullivan. -Ed.

Finis

*"Poor old soldier, poor old soldier, tarred and feathered
and sent to hell, because he didn't soldier well."*
                    -Soldier lyrics to the 'Rogues' March'

He stared unafraid straight into his grave
as he sat on his coffin nearby--
not one of us there formed up in that square
could look the poor boy in the eye.
For each one could see that it might have been he
who had fallen asleep at his post,
but the sleep will now be everlasting...
it's the living who hates this most.

-Pvt. Hell

23

Up Now, Drummer!
~A Cadence~

Drummer boy up at crack of dawn,
get your brogans and britches on,
find those drumsticks, tighten those ropes,
end these sleeping soldiers' hopes
and dreams of seeing home again,
of love and peace and remember when.
Such hopes are hollow as your drum....
Up now drummer, up now, come!

-Pvt. Hell

The fact that a snare drum could cut through the din of a battlefield's raw symphony made this ancient instrument a vital means of communication during the Civil War, the last in which they were used. The two armies mustered tens of thousands of drummer boys, many as young as 11, 12, or 13 years old, who were literally in the thick of the fight, and of whom thousands were killed, wounded, maimed. -Ed.

Fowl Is Fare

All quiet along the Potomac tonight,
except here and there a stray chicken...
who wishes she'd never come into my sight
as I sit here a-pluckin' and pickin.'
It's only a chicken or two, now and then,
but it sets the whole barnyard a-squawkin'...
not a cow, or a mule, or a horse, you old fool,
just the fowl fates of war that we're talkin.'
Almost quiet along the Potomac tonight.

-Pvt. Hell

*A poignant poem about the death of a sentry, "All Quiet Along
The Potomac Tonight" was composed by a New Yorker, Ethel
Lynn Beers, and first published in Harper's Weekly, Nov. 1861.
Shortly thereafter it was set to music by a Rebel officer, John H.
Hewitt, and would become extremely popular on both sides of
the river. Dignity forbids any comparison of Pvt. Hell's version
to the original. -Ed.*

Lucifer's Mist

Smoke of battle, rise you, a sick flower--
into the ether let you send your moment,
nevermore to blow your hot aroma
through the minds of men, and loathing foment.

-*Pvt. Hell*

The Dying Tree, or, I Think That I Shall Ever See

There was a bloody handprint on this tree--
a man stood here (a man unknown to me)
whose Rubaiyat elixir graced this spot...
was it his own, or had his friend been shot?
And was it, then, his final signature,
or did he soldier on to find some cure?
Sweet rain and snow and sun have scoured the bark--
of blood now gone to dust there is no mark,
but in the cool deep glade of memory
there ever shall be blood upon this tree.

-Pvt. Hell

Most every battlefield in this gruesome war featured a tree beneath
which the surgeons placed the most severely wounded to spend their
last moments in the shade. Not surprisingly, the soldiers came to
identify such a spot as 'the dying tree.' As to the immortal "Rubaiyat
of Omar Khayyam," its first English translation dates to 1859. -Ed.

Sweet Tooth

The sutler is the barber here--
he pulled my tooth straight out.
(And yet this is the self-same man
who's giving me the gout.)

He tied a string around the thing
and said: "Be Reb, or Yank?"
If blood and pain were money,
I'd have money in the bank.

-Pvt. Hell

Barbers in the 19th Century also 'practiced' dentistry.
Sutlers sold food, luxuries, and necessities such as alcohol
to the soldiers. -Ed.

A Little Girl's Prayer

Dear God, these horsemen came to our town,
they came and cut all our menfolk down...
I wish I might and I wish I may
hate them until their dying day.

Is it only the gunpowder that I smell,
or some brimstone in which I shall ever dwell?

They killed my father and my brothers...
why did Jesus say, "Do unto others?"
A God who could let this happen to me
must not be the God my father could see.   Amen.

-Pvt. Hell

While atrocities were rife on both sides in Kansas and Missouri,
the ghastly raid by irregular cavalry on the town of Lawrence,
"Bleeding Kansas," saw 185 boys and men of all ages cut down
on their very doorsteps, in front of wives and families, as they tried
to flee their burning homes, farms, and businesses. The raiders
included a youth named Frank James, who would later 'freelance'
with his brother Jesse.   -Ed.

A Soldier's Tail

Our new recruit has four short legs--
we call him Jeff Davis-- see how he begs,
and since he joined our Regiment
we've made him up his own 'dog tent.'
He can't bark as loud as the Sergeant can,
but is a better friend to man--
and if he passed water on the Captain's boots
well, such is the way with all recruits.
He'll even eat our 'salt mule chaw'
(which kills a man when eaten raw)
for he's a loyal little cuss--
even though he caught his fleas… from us!

-Pvt. Hell

*Numerous Civil War regiments were dogged with a canine mascot,
not a few of which were killed in action. The 6th Iowa Volunteers
reportedly sported a "mongrel" who insulted the distinguished
appellation of the President of the Confederacy. -Ed.*

Sharpshooter, Attention!

Well, sharpshooter, now you're in a pinch--
and don't expect us to give an inch,
'cause since we've got you up this tree
we'll teach you a whole new way to see
that War is terrible-- yes, it's true--
when the man in the sights turns out to be you.

-Pvt. Hell

*Snipers, known as sharpshooters during the Civil War, were
generally disliked by the men of both armies for making it
'personal,' and were often killed on the spot when captured. -Ed.*

The Devil's Weed

Oh you Burly! Virginia Weed!
Of all things else you're this army's need.
Reb, take this here coffee, I've had my fill--
who wants to stay jumpy with lungs to thrill?
Just send me a raftload of some of that stuff,
I'll trade you fair up-- it don't have to be snuff!

-Pvt. Hell

*Along with newspapers and the occasional foodstuff, the prime
trading commodities exchanged between northern and southern
soldiers (often lonely pickets facing each other across a river,
and usually against strict orders) were strong Yankee coffee and
fine Rebel tobacco. Trading was often rife when the armies held
truces to bury their dead. -Ed.*

Thinning The Herd

So today marks one year in the army,
'course it wasn't an army then...
we were more of a well-armed rabble
than disciplined fighting men.
But by now all the coffee-coolers and skulkers
and shirkers and stragglers are gone...
so by now, when they bring down a soldier,
something nobler passes on.

-Pvt. Hell

*For once, the Private is being optimistic... there was plenty
of coffee-cooling, skulking, shirking, and straggling to come,
particularly after the warring governments enacted their
military drafts. -Ed.*

Railroad Speculators, or, Raising General Hell

Come on, you brimstone beast, lay on some speed...
200 pounds of pressure's what we need!
We'll give your boiler everything we've got...
We'll get to Chattanooga or be shot!
We'll burn a hundred bridges at both ends...
they'll write about us someday, foes and friends!
So pitch in, boys, and don't you hold your breath!
Break up those cars for wood! We're racing Death!

-Pvt. Hell

In April of 1862, Union spy James J. Andrews and 24 civilian-clothed
Federal volunteers seized a Confederate locomotive (known as The General)
in Big Shanty, Georgia, and headed north; intending to burn bridges, cut telegraph
wires and generally disrupt the Georgia and East Tennessee Railroad lines. In one
of the war's most riveting adventures, they were pursued nearly 200 miles by the
conductor of The General, who had commandeered another engine. But rain-
soaked railway bridges failed to burn, and Andrews and most of his men were run
to ground. The speculator of the 'Great Locomotive Chase' finished his journey not
in Chattanooga, but in Atlanta, where he was hanged as a spy on June 7th, at the
corner of 3rd and Juniper Streets. Andrews was written about, all right, and exciting
motion pictures based on this event were made in 1911(!), 1927, and 1956. -Ed.

Angels' Hare

Last night a rabbit died out in the woods--
they sound so human when they scream, you know.
We couldn't bear the sound, which lit our nerves,
so Jim and I went out to stop the show.
The moon threw vicious shadows at our feet,
the rabbit howled a dirge beyond compare...
thank goodness it was Jim who found the beast.
And when he cooked it up, I got my share.

-Pvt. Hell

The Picket's Midnight

Tall lone pine upon a hill
black against a starry sea,
bayonet poised straight and still
be a sentinel with me.
Like a finger saying Hush
make me listen to my heart…
to the next world I would rush,
from this war let me depart.
What are all these shooting stars?
Deaths, some say, and some say births--
Are there not ten thousand wars?
Are there not ten thousand Earths?

-Pvt. Hell

Reverie Reveille

The farther away that I march each day
the more my thoughts fly to you,
as if all of the moments we've spent apart
are a nightmare need never come true.

I can still see your face in every trace
of the beauty nature reveals…
but the gunpowder taste of this horrible waste
ever into my reverie steals…

I drift on this dream called 'Liberty'
which always ends the same…
the strong will subjugate the weak,
give it any name.

-Pvt. Hell

Fancy This, or, The Roadbed Is Not On The Level

Oh, fancy the comforts of life such as this!
Our rations are hardwood, our coffee is piss.
Our money? What money? Our clothes fall apart.
Our feet are more weary than Abraham's heart.
We go up against guns as big as you please,
and can't see the forest because of our knees.
Our officers know what they know: flowing bowls!
So fancy our comforts, then pray for our souls.

-Pvt. Hell

The phrase 'flowing bowls' was 19th Century slang for copious amounts of alcohol. And might this composition have been a lyric, set to the tune of the 1850's composition "Sweet Betsey From Pike?" We'll never know. -Ed.

O Be Joyful!

O Be Joyful! My skull doth bust!
When we're alone it's you I trust
to light mine eye and calm my nerve,
the things a soldier does deserve.
(I hope this flask has one quaff left
or you shall see me sore bereft)
Yo Ho Be Joyful! You are my cheer--
I'm never alone when you are here.

-Pvt. Hell

O-be-joyful, wobble-water, joy juice, bust-skull, giggle-gargle, brown cow, red-eye, the booz, bang, boiled owl, eau divine... you get the picture; these men could drink. I, for one, am loath to question their motivations. -Ed.

Silent Night, or, Icy Fredericksburg

"Peace on Earth, good will toward men"
the angels sweetly sang...
it was but eighteen centuries ago.
Now on this wicked battlefield
the sun is loath to hang...
so we are going to freeze like flakes of snow.
We wounded are unfortunate
without a rank to show
(God made a host of privates for a reason)
and so my heart is split apart
by icicles of woe
which cannot but reflect upon the season.

-Pvt. Hell

"War does not admit of holidays." -A. Lincoln

Uncle Walt, or, Nature's Chemistry Distill'd

Of course, it isn't much,
but when your life is set to end,
it's mighty sweet to just repeat
your story to a friend…
I found a friend like that:
he looked like 'good St. Nick' himself!
He said, "My name is Walt,"
and took my mail, the big old elf.
We talked awhile, he squeezed my hand,
(I wish I'd felt it though…
my blood was running just a little colder
than the snow.)
So thank you Walter, dear old cuss,
whencever we may roam--
because you cared, I am prepared…
wild Cosmos, be my home.

-Pvt. Hell
  To George Washington Whitman, 51st New York Volunteers,
  and his fellow men wounded at Fredericksburg, December 1862.

Divertisements Musical

So give us our old Brigade Brass Band
and let them play all night...
we'd rather go out with a song in our hearts
if tomorrow we must fight.

Do play the "Mockingbird," "Old Dog Tray,"
and "The Vacant Chair" now, boys--
for even the enemy loves to hear
such haunting sorrows and joys.

Methinks these musicians are red-eyed stiff!
(It's just the way they go...
of course, they can stop a Minié ball
just like any soldier, you know.)

So when your concert's gone and done
let the E-flat cornet
go up on the ridge and play "Home Sweet Home..."
I say nary a heart will forget.

-Pvt. Hell

"I do not think we could have an army without music," remarked Robert E. Lee, and
it can truly be said that these armies marched to the strains of music,
as well as of muscles. Brass instruments were best suited to the rigors of campaigning,
and the war began with thousands of regimental bands, usually composed of between
eight and twelve individuals, which consolidated down to a precious few brigade
bands as the ball wore on. Incidents such as the one described above, and others
in which the opposing armies and bands joined in mutual song and instrumentals,
are documented on several occasions.
So-Do-Mi-So? -Ed.

I Dig It, Proudly

The men call me "Jonah," a Bible name!
I figure it means I deserve acclaim,
since I work harder than anyone
from dawn's early light till day is done.
Each time we pitch camp, before anyone blinks,
I'm detailed to dig the officer's sinks.
They tell me I do the "best job yet!"
Like I wrote home to Ma, I'll never forget.

-Pvt. Hell

"Sinks" was the 19th Century term for latrines. -Ed.

The Barefoot Rank

I am a lowly private,
and grateful every day
that in this vast misjudgment,
I shall have no say.

They can't blame me for starting it,
their hate aroused my hate.
So soon we'll rot and be forgot,
what a stupid fate.

I hope to never answer
for what's bein' said and done…
just put me in the line, boys,
and hand me up my gun.

-Pvt. Hell
To Miss D

The General Respect For Gen'l Lee

Generally speaking,
he's some General,
Gen'l Lee--
in general no General
can general
like he.
For generally, Gen'l Lee
out-generals you,
see?
So Generals generally
respect
Gen'l Lee.

-Pvt. Hell

A Farmer's Lament

The night they burned the covered bridge
I was five miles away.
It's true I tell you, but I see
you care not what I say.
I do not ride for Lincoln,
Davis, Sherman, Forrest, Lee…
I only have a deaf old mule
to keep me company.
But go ahead and hang me then,
my blood be on your brow…
I'll tell the Lord you'll be along
most any moment now.

-Pvt. Hell

A Letter From Her Soldier

I had to go down to the creek after dark
to make myself feel better...
and there as the moon rose over the hill
the stream flowed a little bit wetter.
For in the sweet moonlight I dreamed of you
and your myriad tender charms--
remembering when we were last alone
and how I "presented arms."

-Pvt. Hell

Why Wage War When We Wonder Who's Winning?

Why is it hate has got us by the throat?
Wage slaves to rage, we kill to stay afloat.
War sucks the good out of the purest cause
when into human hearts it sinks its jaws.
We will ourselves to claim God's on our side…
wonder how He'll judge such awful pride.
Who's next, then, to perpetuate Cain's curse?
Winning? Such a word makes matters worse.

-Pvt. Hell

Stonewall's Come Tumbling Down

When ignorant armies clash by night
and ignorant pickets shoot on sight
their burning lumps of lead can be
the doom of genius riding free.

Ol' Blue Lights! Will we see no more
your eye fixed on that distant shore?
Cross over the river, then, and rest...
Marse Robert's right arm did its best.

-Pvt. Hell

*In a tragic (especially for the Confederacy) case of death by
'friendly fire,' Gen'l Thomas J. "Stonewall" Jackson was
brought down by his own troops in the twilight of May 2nd,
1863, the very day of his and Gen'l Lee's audacious triumph
over the troops of Gen'l "Fighting Joe" Hooker in the battle
of Chancellorsville. Gen'l Jackson's electric blue eyes were
said by his men to 'light up' during battle, and his poignant
dying words are well remembered: "Let us cross over the river,
and rest under the shade of the trees." -Ed.*

The Bullet's Song

I am the bullet made for thee
I follow your trajectory:
I feel no meek Jehovah's grace
I only seek the place you pace--

I am the bullet made for thee
I follow your trajectory:
I sing the last refrain you'll hear
I leave it ringing in your ear--

I am the bullet made for thee
I follow your trajectory:
I fly so fast, so far, so true
that NOW! There's nothing you can do.

-Pvt. Hell

As one soldier (no doubt musically-trained) would observe about
the 'refrain' of a bullet: "...it was a swell from E-flat to F, and
as it passed into the distance and lost its velocity, receded to D...
a very pretty change." (Provided it passed into the distance!)
The melody-minded may notice that this 'lyric,' as it were, seems
to dovetail fairly well with the traditional Irish tune "The Minstrel
Boy." -Ed.

Silence Is Gilt, or, A Private's Private Reverie

These officers-- they make me laugh
the way they strut and bray…
there's so few of 'em fit to see
the honorable light of day.

But still, they're good for one thing sure:
they draw the Minié balls!
God, grant their hour upon the stage
…so one less private falls.

-Pvt. Hell

Mars And Venus

All women think they merit to be loved,
so too do soldiers think they will survive,
but nothing shall be fair in love or war,
as we cannot bid Cupid's dart arrive
nor stay the terrible swift sword of Mars--
they pierce hearts good and bad with equal glee.
Are war and love, then, only made for fools?
If you would know, just take a look at me.

-Pvt. Hell
To Ovid

*It is well that the Private chose to dedicate this ditty to the witty
bard of ancient Rome, for the first 8 words of this poem are
clearly 'lifted' from Ovid's immortal "The Art of Love," which
first appeared in 2 B.C. -Ed.*

A Gen'l History Of The Damned Union Army
-As of June, 1863-

The War began with Gen'l Confusion
which soon led to Gen'l Dismay,
and next came Gen'l Reluctance
to use the army in any way…
we then got Gen'l Arrogance
with a saddle for a crown, before the fall,
then sad proof of Gen'l Denial
of any real ability at all.
This was followed by Gen'l Goodtimes,
soon dispelled by a shell (what a shot!)
Does it not seem that Gen'l Disaster
is the one true commander we've got?

-Pvt. Hell

*In chronological order, the lowly Private H defames Generals
Scott, McDowell, McClellan, Pope, Burnside, and Hooker.
Fortunately for the Union army, its next commander, Gen'l
George Meade, (who was appointed by Lincoln mere days
before the battle of Gettysburg) was no general disaster. -Ed.*

Harvest Home

There is a scythe among the bayonets--
the men who see it never say a word...
but surely are their countenances vexed
(these souls ere long unfettered as a bird.)

I never saw the scythe until today,
but ah-- it shines as brightly as the sun.
There is no way to fight this foe, what say?
(How sweetly ineffectual my gun.)

Just now, the scythe is silent as the night,
but oh-- what night is silent, I would ask.
Tomorrow I shall brave the harvest site,
and hope that I stand equal to the task.

-Pvt. Hell

Sergeant Humiston's Farewell

My little children stare at me
from out this picture-frame...
I longed to see them soon again,
be more than just a name.
But fate has ruled another way,
their father shall be no more.
I'll greet them on a brighter day
upon that distant shore.
And while the flames of battle fade
my love burns ever stronger...
Oh, little ones, abide with me
for just a moment longer!

-Pvt. Hell

A nationwide search for the identity of an unknown soldier who
was found dead on the field at Gettysburg, clutching an ambrotype
image of his children, revealed him to be Sergt. Amos Humiston of
the 154th New York Infantry. Sales of "The Children Of The
Battlefield," the winning entry in a contest for a song concerning
this sad but typical story, raised millions of greenbacks to build an
orphans' home in Gettysburg, where Sergt. Humiston's own children
became the first of many residents. -Ed.

Death Watch, or, Just Desserts

Come closer now, soldier, I'm not really dead--
if you touch my watch I'll blow off your head.
I've been watching you rifle the kits of my pards...
I saw you take Joachim's playing cards,
and is that Jefferson's haversack?
As God is my witness, he'll have it back...
and the Colonel's flask-- oh, you are cute.
Well, I may be dying, but I still can...Shoot!

-Pvt. Hell

Breathe Deep, or, The Eyes Have It

If a human birth is a miracle
why not a human death?
'Tis amazing a thing to stop one
as to start a human breath...
Peering into the eye of a dead man
I saw God within his iris--
of a more spiritual epiphany
can any man's soul be desirous?

-Pvt. Hell

Bless Us Father, For We Know What We Do

Ah, Father Corby, do bless us good Father,
for we must go reap the wheat...
and do say a prayer for yourself as well
while the lead and the iron compete.

For you do not carry a weapon, sir,
and trouble be where ye find it--
so when you are done standing up on that rock,
I wish you would sit behind it.

-Pvt. Hell

To the Sons of Erin, 69th N.Y. Vol. Infy., July 2nd, 1863

A statue of Father Corby, still standing upon his rock of ages,
can be found south of the Wheatfield at Gettysburg. -Ed.

58

Nature Of Casualty: Death

I die here where I lie here
and it's strange how calm it seems
as a thousand blood-stained men around me
fill the air with screams...
the smoking choking raging pain
and maelstrom that surround
now fade into a dream
for I'm embraced by loving ground.

Yes, war's a game of chance,
so I surrender up with grace
and as the dying sun
pours its sweet honey on my face,
I look to Minnesota,
say to all of you, Farewell--
remember what we did here,
remember why we fell.

-Pvt. Hell

To the 1st Minnesota Volunteer Infy.

At the behest of Gen'l Winfield Hancock, ("Charge those lines!")
the 262 men of this onetime thousand-man regiment made a virtual
suicide charge against 1,600 'Alabamians' of Wilcox' Brigade in the
smoking sunset of July 2 at Gettysburg. Only 47 'Minnesotians'
were left standing, but they preserved the integrity of the Union line,
(as did the 20th Maine, just to the south at about the same time.)
Said Hancock: "There is no more gallant deed recorded in history."
Said Sergeant Alfred Plummer of Co. K: "We had no time to weep."
-Ed.

Emmitsburg Road, or, Private Haymaker's Muse

I have this heavy feeling in my heart
as though there is already a lead ball here.
And as I look across these amber fields,
I somehow feel I've come this far to fall here.

It seems to be a thousand yards or more…
a thousand yards of shot and shell and hell.
Well, Lord, is this the day you made me for?
I guess the next half-hour's work will tell.

-Pvt. Hell

*Remarked Pvt. William Monte of the 9th Virginia, drawing his
watch from his pocket as the remains of his regiment reached the
Emmitsburg Road while crossing the sun and lead-drenched fields
of Pickett's Charge, and moments before he was struck and killed
by a shell: "We have been just 19 minutes coming." -Ed.*

Double Canister, No Sponging!

Hats off to the Old Dominion boys
who marched up to the muzzles' maw--
I was there on the line on the third of July
and I'll tell you what I saw:
a dozen brave boys of the 53rd
squarely faced the Napoleon's roar--
then all that was left was some smoking shoes
…there just wasn't anything more.

-Pvt. Hell

The 'canister' of the title refers to large tin cans, each packed
with 27 1¼ inch iron balls, which could be blasted point-blank
into oncoming infantry like a giant shotgun. "No Sponging!" refers
to firing in great haste, without the usual wet swab of the barrel to
remove excess powder residue. At Gettysburg, the 53rd Virginia
Regiment reportedly lost 12 or more men from a single such blast
of a 'Napoleon' cannon at the height of Pickett's charge, although
knowledgeable Gettysburg interpreters suggest that the artillery at
that spot were more likely 3-inch Ordinance Rifles, sporting canister
of 110 marble-sized balls, (not that it made much difference to the
men of the 53rd.) -Ed.

Eau de Pickett

'Twas perfume in the General's locks that morn,
but later came aromas much more dear
of sulfer, sweat, and blood rolled into one,
and agony and glory, love and fear--
a mystic, sweet, ethereal, hellish brew
of all the good and bad there is in men,
a whirlwind wafting down the years to come
the fragrant echo of 'remember when.'

-Pvt. Hell

*Gen'l George A. Pickett, who had been appointed to West Point
by onetime Congressman A. Lincoln, commanded only about a
third of the Rebel troops in the famous charge which bears his name
(or which his name bears.) His sweetheart Sally sent him the perfume
with which he loved to dab his long and curly locks. After the war,
Mr. Pickett would sell life insurance.   -Ed.*

Aftermath

I'm light as a feather and smiling like sin,
I'm living and breathing despite the din,
the rage and confusion and horror and pain!
My senses are singing a holy refrain...
God's colors are glorious, luminous, clear...
the mockingbird's lilt thrills my one good ear...
and all terra firma is lit with a glow
the bodies around me will nevermore know.

-Pvt. Hell

Fury And Duty

Upon a time, danced Fury madly in this grass
Upon a time, our shouts rang out above this field
Upon a time, these stones dripped with a heavy dew
Upon a time, the hearts here knew not how to yield.

Upon a time, the wave was dashed upon these rocks
Upon a time, this sky burned hotter than a fire
Upon a time, men knew here love and hate
Upon a time, there was no Duty higher.

~Pvt.Hell

Truth Is Borne Upon The Wind

Oh say, can you smell
the effluvial blight?
O'er the ramparts of hell
her aromas come streaming.
Whose broad plumes of dread fumes
and decomposite airs
of the chosen's dead stares
in our nostrils are steaming.
And the pitiful sight
of the horses' poor plight
gives proof through the night
of the ether's rude might.
Who'll fail to inhale
the sweet fragrance of freedom heaving?
Truth is borne upon the wind:
Bless us Father, we've sinned.

-Pvt. Hell
Gettysburg, July 4, 1863, with apologies to Mr. Key and
his secesh family.

Over 5000 members of the equine species met their demise on
Gettysburg fields. Loyal to their causes to the last, they were also
among the last to be buried, although many were of necessity
cremated in giant pyres of flesh and fencepost. -Ed.

Lincoln Has Stood Up!

Catch the shadow of the man,
if you can, if you can,
get him right there in your lens, while you may.
He will speak for but a minute
packing so much genius in it,
catch his shadow as he casts it, seize the day!

Get your plate carefully coated,
alcohol gun-cotton loaded,
dip it in the silver-- ah, now to the box!
What? The President is done?
Sat him down? Not even one
damned exposure! Dash it all upon the rocks!

-Pvt. Hell

*19th Century photography is a fascinating story in itself... the long
exposures necessary during the war (10-45 seconds) and bulky equipment
of the day making formality the rule, and preventing 'action' photography.
The "plate" referred to is a plate of clear window glass, coated and placed
into a silver solution, then rushed from a darkroom or dark-wagon to a
large wooden camera, where the image had to be exposed within a short time.
Prints on paper could be made from this plate after it was rinsed and dried.
All in all, it was a delicate proposition, requiring artistic virtuosity by the
'operator.' As to Lincoln at Gettysburg, there were at least three photographers
in the vicinity that November day, and in what may be the biggest missed
'photo-op' in photographic history, only one recorded a partial glimpse of the
Great Emancipator, far off in the distance of a large crowd shot. -Ed.*

A Very Good Book

Oh Lord, thou art my shield and my protection…
thy Holy Word hath stopped this Minié ball,
which like a comet came in my direction
as if I had no destiny at all.

But when it's time to call me home, dear Father,
there'll be a newer copy, bound in gold…
not like this steel-clad one my mother gave me,
which by my faith has helped me to grow old.

-Pvt. Hell

The 'Steel-Clad Version' of the Christian Bible
sold particularly well during the 1860's. -Ed.

Maison Vicksburg, 1863

Mule meat, acorns, cane root, grass,
simmered weeds for tea, and rats.
Such is the Cuisine du Jour
for the Vicksburg epicure.
Are you hungry? Do you thirst?
Bone appetit! We'll do our worst!
(On the last of May said I:
"Never shall I eat a worm!")
On July the Fourth I cry:
"Aren't these juicy, plump, and firm?"

-Pvt. Hell

From living in hillside caves to starvation, the good people of
Vicksburg experienced war in all its glorious aspects that long
hot summer. The city and its famished garrison would surrender
on July 4. On that same day, far to the north, Robert E. Lee's
shattered but still defiant army would begin to pull out of
Gettysburg, licking its wounds. -Ed.

Chills The Body, But Not The Soul

Sea, sand, and thunder, oh Jesus I wonder
are You really here in this dying place?
My brothers have been blown to bits in this blunder--
I've gazed on the Great Deceiver's face.
His hot breath set fire to the back of my neck
as his handmaiden Fear weighed my spirit down--
and in this sad ditch where I lay all a-kilter
the tide seeks me out, so I'm going to drown.

"Come Free Men, And Join Us! The Grand 54th!
We'll sunder the shackles for one and for all!"
So while my blood blends with its cousin salt water
I have no regrets that I answered the call.

The sun's disappearing...it's so hard to see now...
the water may sting but it cools where I've bled...
the tide... is it turning? It's turning for me now,
a limpid caress gently cradles my head...
goodbye loving wife, and dear children in Boston,
remember your father when long I've been dead...
and as to you folks who judge men by their color...
perhaps you will see just whose blood's running red...

-Pvt. Hell
 To the fighting 54th Massachusetts Volunteer Infantry,
 Col. Rob't Gould Shaw, and the Douglass family

*While not the first regiment of African-American troops to be raised,
the men of the 54th are justifiably the most famous for their breathtaking
valor at the failed storming of Ft. Wagner, S.C., July, 1863. Two sons
of Frederick Douglass served in the unit. -Ed.*

300 Greenbacks

It's a rich man's war and a poor man's fight
but 300 greenbacks will make it right--
just 300 bills for a 'substitute,'
let that poor fellow learn to shoot
--and be shot at, I hasten to add.
Does the fairness of it make you glad?
It's a poor man's war but a rich man's fight,
to battle his conscience every night.

-Pvt. Hell

Both governments instituted a military draft with unpopular results, perhaps because in the North, a man could pay $300 to purchase the service of a "substitute" soldier, (which was done by at least one future U.S. President) and in the South a man was exempt from the draft if he owned 6 or more slaves. 'Draft riots' occurred, particularly in New York City, where hundreds of lives were lost. "Greenbacks" refer to the green-colored ink first used in 1862 on the reverse of U.S. currency. A few Confederate bills were also printed on the reverse, but in blue. -Ed.

Sheepskin Fiddler

The way he holds them drumsticks and grins,
you would think they came off a chicken...
and the way that he beats that sheepskin, boys,
he really does give it a lickin.'
He wakes the whole regiment straight up
and drums us out into the mud--
but the bullet hole in that damned little drum
sheds nary a drop of blood!

-Pvt. Hell

*Reveille in a Civil War army camp was played on the drum,
not the bugle. The soldiers called drummers 'sheepskin fiddlers,'
although drumheads, or 'batters,' were usually made of calfskin.
Fifers were known as 'straw blowers.' -Ed.*

Food For Thought

Some days we march in quickstep to the west…
some days we march in quickstep to the east…
we try to be quite patient, like a guest
confused as to directions to a feast.

The Generals command: "Move north, move south!"
Each order seems to countermand the last…
which leaves a certain taste within the mouth--
this 'feast' is but a cannibal repast.

-Pvt. Hell

Hell Hotel

I've eaten worms, I've eaten worse,
this 'camp' is cruelty, chapter and verse--
we are not men inside this pen,
just living ghosts recalling when
the world was sweetness, beauty, and light--
before our stinking starving night
of skeletal beasts, of mad despair.
The dead-line beckons everywhere.

-Pvt. Hell

*The term 'deadline,' so painfully familiar to modern readers,
has its origins in the notorious prison camp Andersonville, where
to cross the 'line' and approach the outer stockade perimeter invited
'lead poisoning' from alert young entries perched atop the pine log
walls. Northern and southern prisons alike were examples of hell on
earth, so 'abandon hope' became watchwords for many Civil War
POWs. Upwards of 25,000 Confederates and 25,000 Federals,
Americans all, would not survive their experience in the 'camps.'
-Ed.*

Wounded To The Rear

Well, I got me a red badge of courage,
but I got it on Poltroon Hill--
and each time I sit down to my rations,
I'm reminded with a chill
that if you are going to be wounded
it pays to show your face,
for turning the other cheek, alas,
brings nothing but disgrace.

-Pvt. Hell

"If the Lord gives a man a pair of cowardly legs,
 how can he help their running away with him?"

-A. Lincoln

Down To The Sea In Fits, or, The H.L. Hunley

Land sakes! How I hate this miserable boat--
any fool can see she could never float,
but all my friends will consider me knave
should I not relish a watery grave.

She's already taken three crews down--
that's thirty jewels in her iron crown,
and the clever devil who brought her to be
himself now slumbers under the sea.

Yet I crank, sweat and crank, sweat and crank some more
for here in the darkness we are at war
with the Yankees... and fear... and Poseidon as well...
I just hope there will be some fresh air in hell.

-Pvt. Hell

*The H.L. Hunley, (named after her Rebel inventor, who numbered among
several crews drowned during her sea trials) was the first submarine vessel
to actually sink an enemy ship, the USS Housatonic, this in Charleston
Harbor on the evening of February 17th, 1864. Bearing two officers and
powered by eight sailors turning a crankshaft/propeller, the 25-foot craft,
constructed from a steel boiler, carried a black powder 'torpedo' charge
attached to a long boom on her bow. Either the explosion and resulting
wave swamped the little craft that night, or she was rammed by the Union
warship Canandaigua, but the Hunley's last crew also met with heroic doom.
After spending 130 years submerged in mud at the bottom of the harbor, the
Hunley has been gently raised by her posterity, and is now lovingly displayed
in a poignant museum in Charleston. -Ed.*

Haste Makes Waste

This here's the first steam-powered war,
I hope there's nothing worse--
it's getting so there'll be no point
to sing of War in verse.

For killing ain't so noble now…
hot gases do the deed.
And no one gives a cat's meow,
we just pour on the speed.

-Pvt. Hell

The Girl I'll Leave Behind Me

Oh sweet dear Delilah, come lend me an ear--
I trust that you'll never repeat what you hear,
but when I gaze into your big brown eyes
I feel so enraptured my heart fairly flies.
You listen so patiently to my troubles,
they all float away like gossamer bubbles...
so come hear the secrets I tell no other,
not even my dear sweet sainted mother.
I'd tell you it's love, but I ain't no fool--
It can't be, Delilah, you big dumb old mule.

-Pvt. Hell

Dulce Et Decorum Blest

"Your son was a valiant soldier, ma'am,
and he died from a wound to the head.
He served his land well and we'll miss him,
each one," the Sergeant's letter read.

Yes, that was the truth, but the facts were a bit
more mundane than that letter could tell--
for her soldier boy had been cleaning his gun
in the camp, when Bang! He fell.

-Pvt. Hell

Accidental deaths in the Union Army alone numbered over 4,000.
-Ed.

In God We Bust

No, money cannot mend a heart
(or a nation) sundered and split apart.
It cannot nurture a suckling child
nor pluck the strings of mercy mild.

No, lucre cannot save a soul
or make a farm or village whole.
But should you consider my insights crude--
it's Confederate money to which I allude.

-Pvt. Hell

*Significantly, the printers and engravers who produced the exquisite
currency and postage stamps of the Confederacy (such as the firm
of Keatinge & Ball in Columbia, South Carolina) insisted on being
paid in gold. The good Private would perhaps be amused to know
that the most valuable example of once worthless Rebel currency,
the rare 'Indian Princess' 5-dollar note, is worth as much as
$50,000 in "lucre" to collectors today. -Ed.*

Fish Story

Our Sergeant Kind is a grabblin' man--
he grabbles those fishes like no one can.
Don't need no sinker, line or hook,
he just goes down to the creek 'for a look'
and sticks in his hand, and pulls out a 'plum'
(it surely strikes those fishes dumb
to find themselves caught up that way--
they never have a word to say.)
We'll invite the fish to supper tonight,
their company's always such a delight.

-Pvt. Hell

Who'll Lose More?

Who'll lose more in this blasted war,
the Rebs or the Yanks, you ask?
Jehovah will have to sort that out--
for Him, still a daunting task!

But if you'd know the simple truth
look to this sorry boast:
after what's been spilled and what's been killed,
the Americans lose the most.

-Pvt. Hell

*By the 'best' estimates, Union armies suffered 110,000 battlefield
deaths, and lost another 250,000 to disease. Confederate losses,
though less accurately known, approached 100,000 in combat,
and 165,000 by disease. Of this single 'generation on the march,'
the country lost 625,000 members, each of whom had a heart,
a brain, a future. Death, there is thy sting. -Ed.*

Andersonville Totendanz

Let's do a little jig, me boys,
to celebrate the many joys
of life among the Georgia pines--
We'll promenade! Form two long lines,
let Seamus flay his fiddle gay...
come dance with Death yet one more day!
We scarecrows love to sway and waltz
but while our wardrobe has its faults
and though we're of a single gender
still we step a step so tender
it's enough to leave you weeping.
Lord! What memories we're keeping!
So do a little jig, me boys,
to celebrate the many joys
of life among the Georgia pines--
We'll promenade! Form two dead lines.

-Pvt. Hell

To Pvt. Ezra H. Ripple, fiddler, 52nd Pennsylvania Vol. Infy.

*On at least one occasion, emaciated prisoners waltzed the night
away with a torchlight 'dance on the dead line,' complete with
their own inmate band. What a lovely evening it must have been.
-Ed.*

Rhymes With Lice

There are no lice in paradise,
I go to a better place--
just pitch me down into the ground,
a smile upon my face.
Such earthly torments nevermore
shall taunt this mortal frame--
farewell, you mangy "graybacks,"
I leave you to your game.

-Pvt. Hell

*Lice were the common scourge of all ranks in the Civil War.
Union troops referred to both their insect and human foes alike
using the aforementioned nickname. -Ed.*

It Is Not All Glory

I fight by the light of a crimson moon
with ghosts and with anger and no end soon.
With giants, drenched in each other's blood,
brawling exhausted in the mud.
With childrens' tears, and mothers' pain...
with empty saddles in the rain...
with the hollow place within the heart
where seeds of hatred get their start.
It's not all glory, boys, not quite--
you'll know what else at your very first sight.

-Pvt. Hell

"War isn't hell. It's worse."
–Sergt. Billy Walkabout, Cherokee Nation, US Army Rangers, Vietnam;
Distinguished Service Cross, Purple Heart, 5 Bronze Stars, 5 Silver Stars.
R.I.P. 03-07-2007

Cats And Dogs

Just a little more rain and this refrain
will settle right into the mud--
all these hours of showers induce in my brain
an odd vision of Noah's flood:
for I dream of both armies afloat on the Ark
and the sun has come shining through--
but a sharpshooter downs the white dove with the branch
and the downpour begins anew.

-Pvt. Hell

"And God said unto Noah, The end of all flesh is come before me;
for the earth is filled with violence through them; and behold, I will
destroy them with the earth." -Genesis 6:14 (Steel-Clad Version)

Peace In Pieces
-Christmas Again-

'Peace on Earth, good will toward men...'
if I hear that song sung again,
I wish I may and wish I might
be taken to my silent night!
'Good men in pieces on the Earth'
is what I see, for what it's worth.
So let your angels sing again...
of 'War on Earth, goodbye, Amen!'

-Pvt. Hell

Pain Of Command

General Confusion reigns
giving orders to Kernel Brains,
the commander of Major Disaster,
who's poor Captain Cusser's master.
Lieutenant Underfoot's next,
he leaves Sergeant Barks rather vexed,
soon Corporal Punishment follows--
and beneath all this, Private Hell wallows.

-Pvt. Hell

Bird's Eye View

You know what Joe saw Marse Robert do?
At that last battle, he swears its true--
the General stooped for a little chick
and put it back up in its nest, right quick.
Imagine! The General savin' that bird...
ain't that the strangest thing ever you've heard?

-Pvt. Hell

This incident involving Gen'l Lee is alleged to have occured
under fire on the battlefield of Petersburg, Virginia. -Ed.

Future Tense

There will be locomotives in the sky,
machines that dance, great cities made of glass,
strange ships will plumb Poseidon's deepest lair
(unseen by us-- we shall be leaves of grass.)
The years will come and go and come again
as lovers blow their kisses 'round the world,
and books will talk and cry and laugh and sing
of tonics in which life itself lies curled.
There will be all these things, and many more
fair wonders which we have no language for,
and in the midst of these sweet miracles,
I have to tell you... still there will be War.

-Pvt. Hell

Beyond The Call

"Ah, Duty is as cruel as Death!"
That's what he said, with his last breath--
I wonder what he meant by that?
Is Duty, then, some tight cravat?
Or is it something nobler, pray,
which says to Death: "Come anyway!"

-Pvt. Hell

Lights Out

Blinded by shrapnel! Oh Lord, what a sight--
may I never again suffer such a night.
I was wondering why there was no moon…
when the sun hit my face the answer came soon.
And with it a strange kind of inner light--
at least I'll sleep next to my wife at night.

-Pvt. Hell

Marvellous Mud

'Thrice happy he who, not mistook,
hath read in Nature's mystic book...'

-Andrew Marvell,
ca. 1665

Thrice happy me, here in the mud?
Of Truth in Nature, I've a flood!

-Private Hell,
ca. 1865

*It appears that the lowly Private must have 'picked up'
a volume of poetry somewhere during his travails. -Ed.*

O, Laudanum!

O, laudanum! We know what we know--
just a couple old soldiers up in O-hi-o
just a bottle and a grin and a dose-e-do
we're a grand old pair up in O-hi-o.
No need to ask us what it cost,
at least the Union wasn't lost--
but you and I we got our fill.
Thank God the pension pays the bill.
Ah, morphine! We know what we know--
just a couple old soldiers up in O-hi-o.

-Pvt. Hell

Laudanum, a bracing cocktail of alcohol and opium, was
the era's supreme painkiller, and its use resulted in the wide
range of personal and social effects which might be expected
from such a brew. Civil War soldiers were also among the
first to be injected with a new 'wonder drug,' the opiate morphine.
Those unfortunates who became addicts were said to suffer from
"army disease." -Ed.

Spirit Whirled

My muse? She wanders the battlefield,
the one in the human heart--
where the struggle lasts forever
as we tear ourselves apart.

Where a life accounts for nothing,
where there's glory all around...
right until the sorry moment
when they lay you in the ground.

My muse, she looks not right nor left
but fades from scene to scene...
her wistful smile cloaks all the while
the fury in her spleen.

-Pvt. Hell

Appomattox Epitaph

"I'd rather face a thousand deaths...."
Is that what Marse Robert said?
And all of us held our puny breaths,
and we each of us hung our head.

-Pvt. Hell

*Robert E. Lee reportedly made this remark to his aides as he
left his tent to surrender to Ulysses S. Grant on Palm Sunday,
April 9th, 1865. Not long after in Washington City, on the
balcony of the White House, Abraham Lincoln would request
the serenading U.S. Marine Band play "Dixie," pronouncing it
"fairly captured" and one of his "favorite tunes." -Ed.*

New Faces Greet Thee

If the stork be avenger of adultery
such could explain this babe I see--
for I've been one of Sherman's boys
lo, these two years! Such are the joys
of being a soldier, I suppose.
Well, come then, wife, and hold me close.

-Pvt. Hell

"To console ourselves for all those things, happily we still
have adultery! Maryland tobacco! And Spanish cigarette
paper!" -French writer Petrus Borel, in "Rhapsodies,"
ca.1850

Cross Purposes
-Black Easter, 1865-

Jesus Jesus, how you please us...
haunt, defy, cajole and tease us,
(not to mention all the strife
engendered by one human life.)
But whether as a God or man
you live beyond your mortal span.

-Pvt. Hell

*One might ruminate upon exactly where Pvt. H found himself
on this holy (and unholy) week's end... which saw not only the
raising of the Stars and Stripes above the rubble of Ft. Sumter
after precisely four long years of fratricidal bloodshed, but
President Lincoln's assassination (a day which a shocked
generation would forever remember as "Black Easter.") -Ed.*

Our American Cousin

I am the bitter little pill
of lead and antimony
who works with Mr. Deringer's assistance.
Tonight I'm at the theatre
to ring a curtain down,
for flesh and bone to me hold no resistance.
I'll be a shot heard round the world!
My tiny flight shall tell!
My echo will belong now to the ages…
and no pound of prevention
shall be worth my ounce of hate.
For all this great man's works, I am the wages.

-Pvt. Hell

H. Deringer, Philadelphia gunsmith, invented the particularly small firearm which came to be known, mispelled as it is, by his name. The single most notorious example of his handiwork can be seen today in the haunting museum at Ford's Theater in Washington, DC. -Ed.

Bon Voyagee

Time is an ocean which ebbs and flows
with currents, eddies, shoals--
and Love the emotion which Time well knows
sails hither and yon with our souls.

-Pvt. Hell

So go and consider eternity, if it's in your power,
but just how much longer will you live than this flower?
-Ed.

Heavenly Perdition

Ignorant,
I asked God:
"If you are omnipotent, omniscient, and omnipresent,
how can there be a Hell?"

And God said:
"Hell is where I am not… hence, in Hell,
I disguise myself as the Devil."

"Holiday in Hell?" said I.
"Paradox in Paradise," said He.

-Pvt. Hell

There is an element about some poetry which is able to make even physical suffering and death cheerful things to contemplate and consummations to be desired.

–Mark Twain, *Post-Mortem Poetry,* 1870

...I have met them, I say, not seldom in the army, in camp, and in the hospitals. They are often young men, obeying the events and occasions about them, marching, soldiering, fighting, foraging, cooking, working on farms or at some trade before the war-- unaware of their own nature (as to that, who is aware of his own nature?) their companions only understanding that they are different from the rest... more silent, "something odd about them," and apt to go off and meditate & muse in solitude.

–Walt Whitman, *Specimen Days,* 1863

THE MAN ON THE COVER

Graciously standing in for the cover portrait of Private Hell is the Editor's great-great-great uncle, Pvt. Alonzo C. Hayden of Co. D, 1st Minnesota Volunteer Infantry. (Hence, the trefoil 'clover' insignia he wears refers not to Ireland, but rather the 2nd Corps of the Army of the Potomac.) Alonzo was born in Maine in 1839, and emigrated in 1854 with his preacher father and family to Champlin, Minnesota, near today's Lake Hayden.

Through a fluke of fate, Private Hayden became one of the first men to volunteer for the war; Minnesota Governor Alex. Ramsey happened to be in Washington, in the office of Sec'y of War Simon Cameron, when news of the shelling of Ft. Sumter arrived via telegraph. Ramsey immediately tendered a thousand volunteers from Minnesota to help "put down the rebellion." His offer accepted by Lincoln, Ramsey wired home and Alonzo, age 22, who happened to be sitting on the courthouse steps in Anoka as the news spread, jumped up and signed on in mid-April, 1861.

Pvt. Hayden's story is as sadly typical as his eyes are haunted; he saw the elephant, sure enough, fighting in most of the large battles of the first half of the war, eventually winding up in a hospital in Washington City in the spring of 1863. Fate being capricious, he recovered sufficiently to rejoin his regiment as they marched off into the searing summer heat... northward, to the peaceful little Pennsylvania town of Gettysburg.

As it did for many other Americans, the war ended there for Private H... He can be found buried amidst a large number of his Minnesota compatriots in Gettysburg's lovely National Cemetery, where the poignant, immortal and now-revered words of Abraham Lincoln floated over their deaf ears on a cold November day in 1863.

--S.B.

*The Editor wishes to gratefully thank those who have accompanied him
~whether literally or not~ on various Civil War sojourns, so in no
particular order of importance (all being important)
heartfelt appreciation and salutations to:*

James B. Hendricks, Paul M. Carter, Jr., James D. Owens, Jay Ungar, Terry Hall, Steve Sylvia, Nancy Dearing Rossbacher, Sally Anderson & Frank LaBreck, Elaine Katuin, Arn Kind, Claudia Kunin, Daniel Binder, Stephen & Wendy Osman, Kip Noschese, Robert Lee Hodge, Edwin C. Bearss, Bill & Mona Haiber, Huell Howser, Ken Burns, Kim Sebestyen, Cricket Pohanka, Don Troiani, Ray Bradbury, Richard Moe, James Goble, Steve "OK" Knowles, Dave "Doubleday" Margolis, Col. Pete Barnett USMC, Dan Munson, Miller Breese, Bill Huntington, Paul Penrod, Charles Pinkham, Bob Gresh, Garrison Keillor, Doug Cooper, Andrew Endsley, Sean Malis, Victoria Molcsany, "Dr. Freddy" Fennell, Gabor S. Boritt, Paula Boger, Dennis Fuller, Paul Arentz, Steve & Karl Harness, Wm. A. Frassanito, Simon E. Spalding, Pierre King, Luke Bjerke, Clive Henrick, Jeff Daniels, Josh & Randy Henniger, Shelby Foote, Andre Rigdon, Dr. Robt J. & Kathy McKenna, Dr. Cary Gota, Lisa Hineman RN AVN, Carl Clink, Erica Martinez, Ian Frazier, Tony Horwitz, Bradley White, the Tillman family, Roger Wilson, Billy Agnew, Jerry Ernst, Mark Elrod, Jeff Peters, Wayne Jorgenson, Charles Baudelaire, E. A. Poe, S. A. Griffin, L. A. Bogen, S. L. Wade, W. H. Auden, C. T. Howell, Miss S. Williams, Dean Mora, Dan Woolpert, Mike Bogert, Walter Nelson, Paul Flemming, Crystal Weinhold, Kyle Thompson, Cameron Larson, Robert Westbrook, Pierre King, Keith Gulsvig, Wayne Pierce, William C. Davis, Bruce Catton, LuAnn Mason, Donna Castor, Interpretive Rangers Bert Barnett & Evangelina Rubalcava-Joyce at Gettysburg, Kathleen Shaputis and the devoted artisans at Gorham Printing in Washington State, & finally, The Band of the California Battalion;
(music from a day when instruments had character & characters had instruments)
Maestro Gary Thomas Scott, Lawrence Schmahl, Randall Silvers, Rich Snyder, Sidney Hopson, Dave Williams, Lon Dimmit, Dave Linson, Bill Craven, Sid Viles, Jeff & Shannon Haberman, Vykee, Sheldon, & Aaron Gordon, Jeffrey Levine, Rich Candelaria, Andy Figge, and Wayne Wright. You guys can really blow a tune!

*Affectionate thanks as well to the amazing extended Bartel family of artists, writers,
musicians, scholars, poets, archaeologists, bibliophiles, spiritual comforters,
and downright upstanding folk of whom I am so
fortunate and proud to be a member...
love you, Kate & Wyatt,
Bruce & Carol.*

ABOUT THE EDITOR

The editor, left, on the set of
Steven Spielberg's *Amistad.*
Photo by Claudia Kunin.

Steven Bartel is a native of Minnesota whose
first impressions of the American Civil War
era were formed as a youth during the exciting
and ubiquitous centennial era of 1961-1965.
To his great good fortune he learned to play
percussion instruments at a tender age, thereby
inculcating early a love for metered verse.

Mr. Bartel is an avid reader and writer, has
designed graphics for the entertainment industry in Los Angeles for many years, and enjoyed
the pleasure of appearing in several feature
films as a 19th-century reenactor. (Huzzah! for
the 20th Maine!) He is also a humble 'sheepskin fiddler' in the popular "Band Of The
California Battalion," a West Coast historical
brass band of some note.

This is Mr. Bartel's first known published
manuscript, accordingly, he salutes those hardy
readers who have carried on so nobly to...
The End.

For permission to use Private Hell's compositions for easily-mounted community or
school theatrical presentations, as song lyrics, to order copies of this book or inquire
about multiple purchases for educational institutions or US military personnel at home
or abroad, please contact the publisher for generous terms.

HELLBOUND PRESS
PO Box 65073 Los Angeles, CA 90065-0073
323-982-9060 (Mon-Fri 9-5 PST)

A tithe from this book goes to the Civil War Preservation Trust (www.civilwar.org) to help preserve
and protect the hallowed grounds of the Civil War era. Join us!
A short excerpt of Mr. Pohanka's foreward has been quoted with permission in a Time-Life publication.